Rhyme Time

Written by Charlotte Raby

Illustrated by Abhilasha Khatri

Collins

2

4

6

8

11

13

Can you say these rhymes?

🐾 Review: After reading 🐾

Read 1: Phonemic awareness

- Play 'find it!' by looking for the items in the small circles at the bottom of the pages, to build phonemic awareness. Choose an object or two per page and ask the children to find them in the illustration. Emphasise the initial sound of each word and then say the word. (e.g. Can you find a ttt teapot?)

- When they have found the object, ask the children to say the first sound of the word.

- Look at pages 14 and 15 together and ask the children to say and act out the rhymes.

Read 2: Vocabulary

- Encourage the children to hold the book and turn the pages.

- Spend time looking at the pictures and discussing them, drawing on any relevant experience or knowledge the children have. Encourage them to talk about what they can see in each picture, giving as much detail as they can. Expand the children's vocabulary by naming objects in the illustrations that they do not know.

- Sound-talk an object or two from the circles at the bottom of each page. (e.g. Can you find the d-o-g?) Sound-talk but do not blend the word. When the children find the object, encourage them to blend the word.

Read 3: Comprehension

- Read the book again. Ask:
  - Which animals jump on the bed? (*monkeys*) What does their mummy do? (*phone the doctor*)
  - What is down at the station? (*the little puffer trains*)

A list of rhymes shown in the book:

p2	Ten Little Monkeys; Polly Put the Kettle on;	p9	Pop Goes the Weasel; I am the Music Man;
p3	Ten in the Bed; I'm a Little Teapot;	p10	Miss Molly Had a Dolly; Teddy Bear, Teddy Bear;
p4	B-I-N-G-O; A Sailor Went to Sea, Sea, Sea;	p11	Sleeping Bunnies; Head Shoulders Knees and Toes;
p5	Dingle Dangle Scarecrow; Five Little Speckled Frogs;	p12	See Saw Margery Daw; Ring-a-ring o' Roses;
p6–7	Down by the Station; The Wheels on the Bus;	p13	Row Row Row Your Boat; Two Little Dickie Birds.
p8	Pat-a-Cake; One, Two, Buckle My Shoe;		